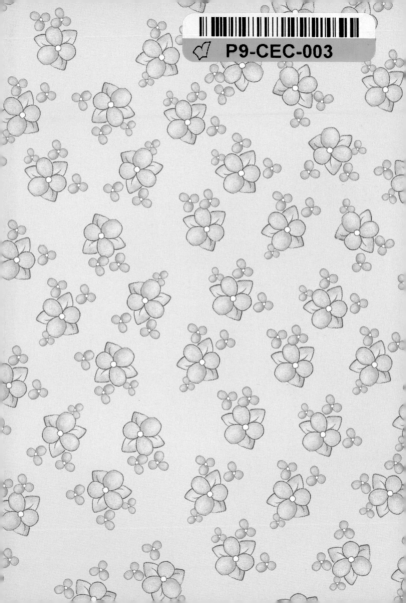

P9-CEC-003

The Precious Moments Of Easter

by Angela Grace
Illustrated by Samuel J. Butcher

BALLANTINE BOOKS
NEW YORK

A Ballantine Book
Published by The Random House Publishing Group
© 2004 by Precious Moments, Inc.
Licensee: The Random House Publishing Group,
a division of Random House, Inc. All rights reserved.

All rights reserved under International and Pan-American
Copyright Conventions. Published in the United States by
The Random House Publishing Group, a division
of Random House, Inc., New York, and simultaneously
in Canada by Random House of Canada Limited, Toronto.

Precious Moments is a registered
trademark of Precious Moments, Inc.

Ballantine and colophon are registered
trademarks of Random House, Inc.

www.ballantinebooks.com

Library of Congress Cataloging-in-Publication Data
is available from the publisher upon request.

ISBN 0-345-46207-6

Book design by Julie Schroeder

Manufactured in the United States of America

First Edition: March 2004

1 3 5 7 9 10 8 6 4 2

*O*ur lives are
made up of Precious Moments.

Sometimes they are part of a celebration like
a birthday, a wedding, or a graduation.

Sometimes they involve school or
maybe our friends or family.

These moments are precious because they remind
us of the most important things in life.

But sometimes these moments are extra special.
They involve events that are bigger and more
important than our lives on Earth.

Sure they also involve delightful traditions
for children, some ritual reenactments,
and even joyful family reunions.

But Easter is more than just the sum of all of
these things—it is the celebration of rebirth.

These are the Precious Moments of Easter.

*D*o you remember . . .

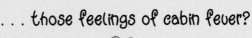

. . . those feelings of cabin fever?

The weather had kept you indoors all winter, and you
were yearning for some wide-open spaces.
Through your bedroom window, you'd seen hints of
sunshine only to have the clouds and rain reappear.
You were ready to run, jump, and play, but the
weather wouldn't cooperate.
Springtime was on its way.

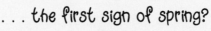

. . . the first sign of spring?

Maybe it was a bit of green slipping through a patch of
melted snow, or maybe it was as simple as the
sight of newly hatched baby birds snuggled in
their nest.

Whether it was the fragrance of a coming April shower or
filling an Easter basket with sweet treats, you were
certain spring had finally arrived!

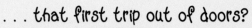

. . . that first trip out of doors?

You still needed a sweater or even a light jacket to keep
warm, but there was no mistaking how great it felt
to be outside again.

The warmth of the sun, the freshness of the air . . . everything was coming alive around you.

. . . when you began to value the wondrous gift of nature?

You had learned in school all about the natural beauty that exists around the world, and all of the amazing creatures that inhabit it.

You also learned that you were a part of it.

You were as much a part of the earth as the seas, the forests, and the skies—a living, breathing part of nature.

And as the world reawakened in the spring, you couldn't help but be awed by the glory of its manifest.

. . . the sweet songs of spring?

You may not have even noticed the birds had quietly
    flown south for the winter and the air outside was
    silent and still. But come spring when the birds
    suddenly reappeared, singing their joyous melodies,
    you realized how much you had missed their
    sweet music.
Even more treasured after a prolonged absence, the
    beautiful symphony of nature is always welcome.

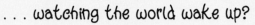

. . . watching the world wake up?

Many of nature's wonders hibernate.

Plants stay underground to keep warm, and come to
life when they feel the sun's rays on the earth
above them.

Some animals curl up in their burrows during winter,
sleeping the cold days away with little snacks of
nuts and berries that were saved during the
previous summer.

The spring season is wake-up time, and everyone has a
role to play as nature comes alive again.

. . . the first shower of spring?

They say that April showers bring May flowers, and even
the worst spring rain is a welcome relief from the
cold of winter.

The rain comes in and waters the ground, nurturing the
seeds and buds that fell to Earth in autumn.

There is also something charming about a spring rain,
especially when you have a trusty yellow slicker, a
big umbrella, and most important, the companion-
ship of a great friend.

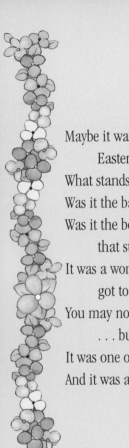

. . . your first Easter?

Maybe it wasn't really your first Easter—just the first
      Easter that you remember.

What stands out in your mind?

Was it the baby birds or the fresh flowers of spring?

Was it the bountiful baskets or the snow white bunnies
      that supposedly delivered them?

It was a wonderful time of family magic where everybody
      got together in his or her Sunday best.

You may not have understood exactly what was going on
      . . . but you knew it was important.

It was one of the most important days of the year.

And it was a happy Easter.

. . . your favorite stuffed bunny?

You probably don't remember when it first came into
your life, though you might remember who gave it
to you: a grandparent, a dear aunt, or maybe an
old friend of the family.

It felt so soft and cuddly and it quickly became your best
friend.

Soon you realized that bunnies meant Easter—whether
as a stuffed animal, a chocolate candy, or a real
one on the farm.

. . . when you always tried
to do what your parents wanted?

You weren't perfect.

You tried to pay attention but sometimes got distracted,
and sometimes you didn't really listen at all.

There was always so much going on when you were
little, especially on Easter morning.

You just wanted to eat yummy candy chicks and hunt
for eggs in the garden . . . but your parents wanted
you to go to church. As always, they knew what
was more important.

That's why they're your parents.

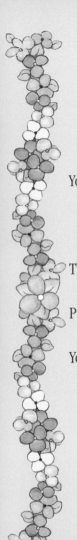

. . . when you gradually began to understand the importance of going to church?

You began to pay attention, not just to the singing
   of songs and the colorful clothes everyone was
   wearing . . . you began to listen to the words that
   everyone would say together.
They were prayers, just like the ones you said each night
   when you went to bed.
Praying is a way of talking to God, and nowhere was it
   more appropriate than in His house: church.
You prayed, you listened, and you learned.

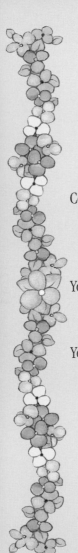

. . . when you got a little older
and you began to question
if the Easter bunny
really existed?

Cotton-tailed and snow white, the bunnies were still very
 much a part of the wonderment of nature that
 came to life each spring. But somehow they were
 just a bit less magical.

You no longer believed that they delivered baskets of
 chocolate eggs and marshmallow chicks each
 Easter morning.

You knew then that there was so much more to Easter
 than you had realized.

. . . when you began to notice that the most important part of Easter took place on Sunday morning?

Everybody would wake up and get dressed in his or her Sunday best.

New hats for the mommies, and nice suits for the daddies.

Of course, later in the day your family would gather for a festive meal, followed by a candy feast of chocolate bunnies and cream-filled eggs.

But first things first.

Everyone had to go to church. There you realized that it was the quiet solemnity and joy of the service that truly makes this day special for your whole family.

It was Easter, after all.

... that time you wanted to stay home instead of going to church?

A big basket of treats had been delivered while you were
sleeping, and your grandparents had just given
you a cute stuffed bunny.

Everything was there, ready and waiting for your
enjoyment.

You went to church every Sunday.

But Easter was something special.

Surely it would be all right to stay home just this once.
After all, it was Easter . . . but your parents didn't
agree.

And while you were at church surrounded by your family,
you realized that your parents were right, that it
was especially important to go to church because
it was Easter.

The bunnies and sweets would just have to wait.

28

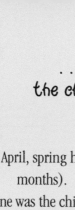

... when you noticed the changes in the seasons?

By April, spring had come to stay (at least for a few months).

Gone was the chill of winter, and a new year was now officially well under way.

Spring was here, summer would soon follow, and the entire world was beautiful and alive as nature woke up from its winter slumber.

Soon the glory of green would give way to a magnificent rainbow of colors all around you.

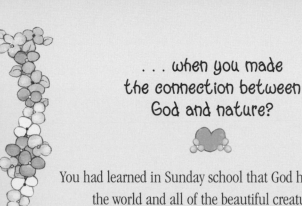

. . . when you made the connection between God and nature?

You had learned in Sunday school that God had made
the world and all of the beautiful creatures that
inhabited it.

You also learned how to pray . . . how to talk to God.
You knew He was always listening.

He had done so much for the world, for *you*. . . . Prayer
was just one of the ways you could give thanks for
His gifts.

As the world reawakens in the spring, you can't help but
be awed by the glory of His creations.

. . . trying to help nature along?

You wanted to be a good sower too.

Maybe your first experience was planting a seed in a milk
carton or perhaps on Grandma's farm or in your
own backyard. You knew that you had to take good
care of the sprout or else it would never grow big
and strong.

And there you were on your hands and knees, doing
your duty.

You cared for it, paid attention, making sure it had
plenty of sunshine and water. And with your love,
it grew.

. . . collecting eggs
for the Easter festivities?

You tried not to disturb the nest on your grandma's farm
 too much, but the chickens and the geese got in
 your way nonetheless.

You thought back for a moment to when you were
 younger, and how you used to think that the
 Easter eggs were always that way, and that the
 Easter bunny delivered them at the crack of dawn
 on Sunday morning.

But this was fun too.

In fact nothing was more special than gathering and
 decorating eggs for Easter with Grandma. And
 after the job was done, she would always make
 you a freshly baked batch of cookies, made with
 her special ingredient: love.

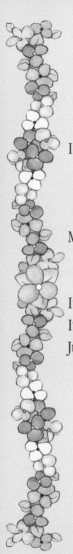

. . . the first Easter basket that you helped put together?

It was made out of straw and whicker, and the colored eggs rested on a bed of green grass. Perhaps there was a chocolate bunny and maybe a candy chick, too.

Maybe you made the basket for a friend or as a gift for your mom or dad . . . or maybe you just made it for yourself.

It was your very own creation.

It was your own basket and you were proud.

Just the way your parents were proud of you.

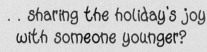

. . . sharing the holiday's joy with someone younger?

Maybe it was your brother or sister or perhaps a younger cousin or neighbor. They believed in the Easter bunny and didn't really understand the significance of this special day.

They were still little . . . but you knew that they could now take part in the more meaningful traditions of the holiday as well.

You let them pitch in with the decorating and sharing of the eggs and all of the other customs of Easter.

. . . not quite always living up to your potential?

As you got older you prided yourself on being more
      mature, and you always tried to set a good example,
      particularly for the younger ones.

You realized that you had to act more grown-up on the
      inside as well, perhaps denying yourself sweets
      prior to Easter as a small sacrifice in commemora-
      tion of Lent.

And sometimes you fell short of your goal.

We are all human and imperfect and God knows this.

He appreciates the effort and the sacrifice and knows you
      will try harder next time.

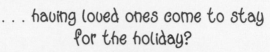

. . . having loved ones come to stay
for the holiday?

Around Easter time, you knew they'd arrive—cousins,
aunts, uncles, and family friends. You looked
forward to the familiar sound of a car pulling up,
and the smiling faces that would pour out.

Easter time meant more friends would be there. More
kids to play games with, and more adults to tell
your favorite Easter stories.

After dinner, everyone would gather around to spend time
together and catch up. It didn't matter if you got
sleepy and had to be carried off to bed. You knew
that your guests would still be there in the morning;
sharing a big breakfast before church. When you
got up and went into the kitchen, you'd see so
many people to love.

And so many people who loved you.

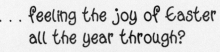

*. . . feeling the joy of Easter
all the year through?*

Seasons come and go, and the gentleness of spring
        makes way for the heat of summer, the cool of fall,
        and the cold of winter, before arriving full circle
        back to the promised rebirth of a new year.
No matter how cold the chill or foreboding the winds, we
        always know that spring is just around the corner,
        the sun waiting to warm us with its light.

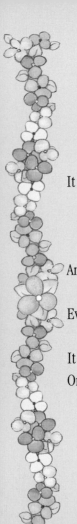

. . . the great Easter dinners you used to share with your family?

It was different from Thanksgiving. There was always plenty of food, but it was never the type of feast that made you want to take a nap in order to sleep away the feeling of overindulgence.

And the requisite turkey was usually replaced by some other fabulous dish.

Everybody was still dressed in his or her Sunday best, and no one seemed distracted by sports on TV.

It was a different sort of holiday family meal.

One might even say that it was a holy day family meal, and that made all the difference.

. . . when you realized that not all
angels live in heaven?

People who dedicate their lives to helping others are also
   angels.

Doctors, nurses, and teachers all do God's work on earth.

Good deeds are the best way to prepare for the glory of
   Easter. When these deeds are done for strangers, or
   for those less fortunate than yourself, then your
   actions are truly angelic.

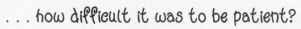

. . . how difficult it was to be patient?

Do you remember how the hours used to drag when you
were younger, particularly when you knew that
something good was coming just over the horizon?
Even if the wait was only a few hours, it felt like an
eternity.
The Easter-egg hunt and the other games weren't
scheduled until later in the afternoon. You didn't
think you could possibly wait any longer.
But you had to and you did.
In the end, the anticipation was half the fun.

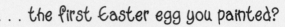

. . . the first Easter egg you painted?

You were finally old enough to decorate an Easter egg all by yourself. You took extra time to make sure it was exactly right. Pink, green, yellow, and light blue—you wanted your egg to have every single color.

Maybe your lines weren't as even as those of your older brother or sister, but you didn't care.

You were decorating it on your own, and it was the most beautiful egg you had ever seen.

. . . picking wild flowers in the meadow?

You were with your best friend or maybe your brother or sister.

Your mother had given you the very important job of collecting flowers to decorate the table for Easter Sunday.

The flowers had just begun to bloom in all sorts of beautiful colors. You picked each flower with thought and care, wanting the bouquet to reflect the blessedness of the day.

And it did.

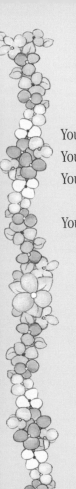

. . . seeing your first rainbow?

You were awed by its magical beauty.

You couldn't tell where it began or ended.

You wanted to reach out and touch it, but it disappeared
before your very eyes.

Your mother told you that the rainbow was sent especially
to you by an angel high up in the clouds—one of
the many beautiful gifts of the spring season.

. . . the women who cared for you when you were young?

Mothers, sisters, aunts, and friends all played an important part in your life.

They loved and cared for you and helped you to grow into the fine adult that you later became.

Just like the little plant you tended in the garden, they tended you.

This is just one of the things that make them so special.

(And maybe it's the reason that Mother's Day is a spring celebration, too!)

. . . finding out that people celebrate Easter everywhere?

When you celebrate Easter, there are people everywhere
celebrating with you, not just in the town where
you grew up, or where you live now. Sometimes
our different cultures or the different ways people
look make it easy to forget how similar we are.
Different flowers grow in different gardens, and no one
egg is painted exactly like another. That's what
makes springtime so joyous and full of color. God
sees the beauty in everyone; the love for Him they
share with one another.
Isn't Easter better because the world celebrates it together?

Your mother would help you pick it out each year—pink
or yellow or green, with fancy matching shoes.
Once it was on, you felt older, almost as pretty as your
mom. Your hair was done up or curled the way
grown-ups wore it. You tried so hard to keep
your new dress clean as you tiptoed through the
garden, feeling as pretty and delicate as a spring
flower.
On the way up the church steps, seeing everyone in their
Sunday best made you feel proud. There was something important about your new dress; it made you
feel different from the way you felt getting dressed
up for a party or a special event. Making sure you
looked nice was one of the ways you showed your
respect.

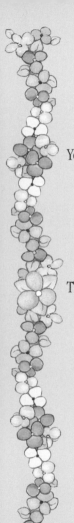

. . . when you first believed in miracles?

You saw a baby chick hatch for the very first time.
Perhaps it was at your grandmother's farm, or
maybe in school or at a local petting zoo. As
the fragile shell broke away to reveal the small
newborn, you realized that you were observing the
miracle of life.

The spring season is a special time of year when little
miracles can be seen everywhere.

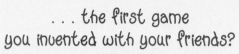

. . . the first game
you invented with your friends?

You had all afternoon to play outside and you could
make up the rules. Only you and your friends
could know them; it was your secret code.

Like the happy chirps birds use to talk to one another on
sunny days, the secrets of the game you played
were yours to keep, or to teach to new friends along
the way.

Maybe you don't remember the exact rules anymore, but
you know that you won.

Everyone won, because you played it together.

*. . . when you first
gave a special Easter gift?*

Helping your mother wrap the chocolates in colorful
cellophane and tucking them into the basket, you
knew you were doing something special.

The big-handled basket was heavy in your small arms.
But as you carried it down the walk to your
neighbor's house, the feeling in your heart made
it light. You knew that your neighbor's family
couldn't be with them for this holy day. What they
needed was a little angel to remind them that
Easter meant caring.

That angel was you.

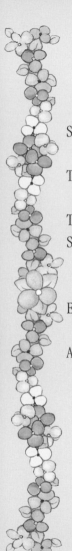

. . . learning the Bible stories?

Some you heard at Sunday services, others at your
mother's knee.

They were different than the normal bedtime stories of
talking animals and grand adventures.

These stories were meant to instruct as well as entertain.

Some were parables, others were events from biblical
history and still others were incidents from the life
of Christ.

Even though He was the Son of God, He still lived much
of His life on Earth the same way as you and me.

And that is why His life is a lesson for us all.

. . . the story of the good shepherd?

It was one of your favorite stories to hear during the
Easter season. Maybe you heard it for the first
time from your mother or at church during
Sunday school.

You learned that Christ is the good shepherd and we are
His sheep, helpless without His guidance. He leads
us along the right paths.

You felt safe and protected, knowing He'd be there for you.

. . . being prepared?

Spring is a season of surprises.

The weather can change quickly without warning,
and holidays like St. Patrick's Day, Easter, and
Memorial Day seem to come and go. The demands
of the school year increase as the semester draws to
a close.

There is no greater feeling than being prepared for what
life has in store for you, whether it is a sudden rain
shower or a pop quiz.

A little preparation can go a long way.

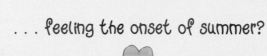

. . . feeling the onset of summer?

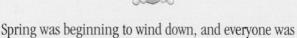

Spring was beginning to wind down, and everyone was staying outdoors.

There were picnics and fairs to attend, games to play, and family fun to enjoy.

You were chosen to be Spring Queen or Lord of the May as part of all the wonderful festivities that were whizzing by.

Spring was coming to an end, school would soon be over, and in no time, summer would arrive in all its glory.

Easter is a time to remember.

In the spring the earth awakens. Once again it grows full of hope and promise, shedding the cold and quiet of winter.

As we come together for Easter, we celebrate this renewal by sharing familiar traditions with those we love. So many people and events have shaped our lives and made us who we are today.

Over each passing year it is important to be thankful for having arrived here. For though our traditions remain the same, Easter is a time to create new memories.

Remember the past, but also enjoy the *precious moments* of today.

 Angela Grace